Let's Work Together

by Kyla Steinkraus

Content Consultants:
Melissa Z. Pierce, L.C.S.W.
Sam Williams, M.Ed.

Rourke
Educational Media

rourkeeducationalmedia.com

Teacher Notes available at
rem4teachers.com

www.rourkeeducationalmedia.com

Melissa Z. Pierce is a licensed clinical social worker with a background in counseling in the home and school group settings. Melissa is currently a life coach. She brings her experience as a L.C.S.W. and parent to the *Little World Social Skills* collection and the *Social Skills and More* program.

Sam Williams has a master's degree in education. Sam Williams is a former teacher with over 10 years of classroom experience. He has been a literacy coach, professional development writer and trainer, and is a published author. He brings his experience in child development and classroom management to this series.

PHOTO CREDITS: Cover: © kate_sept2004; page 3: © Agnieszka Kirinicjanow; page 5: © Deborah Cheramie; page 7: © Pamela Moore; page 8: © kali9; page 9: © mayo5; page 11: © mümin inan; page 12: © Bart Coenders; page 13: © kali9; page 15: © kristian sekulic; page 17: © Doug Berry; page 18: © Miroslav Georgijevic; page 19: © Chris Bernard; page 20: © kali9

Illustrations by: Anita DuFalla

Edited by: Precious McKenzie

Cover and Interior designed by: Tara Raymo

Library of Congress PCN Data

Let's Work Together / Kyla Steinkraus
(Little World Social Skills)
ISBN 978-1-61810-135-8 (hard cover)(alk. paper)
ISBN 978-1-61810-268-3 (soft cover)
Library of Congress Control Number: 2011945278

Rourke Educational Media
Printed in the United States of America,
North Mankato, Minnesota

rourkeeducationalmedia.com

customerservice@rourkeeducationalmedia.com • PO Box 643328 Vero Beach, Florida 32964

Have you ever worked with someone else on a **project**?

Working together is when two or more people **cooperate** to complete a job or project.

If you work together, you are part of a team. You work towards the same **goal**. **Teamwork** is a part of many jobs.

A coach and the players work together when they play a game.

Pilots and air traffic controllers work together to make sure airplanes land safely.

Authors and illustrators work together to create a book. The author writes the story. The illustrator paints or draws the pictures.

You can finish the job faster if you have a friend helping you.

You can divide the work to make it go faster. You can use another person's **talents** to help finish a project.

Can you think of a project you could work on with a friend?

Sometimes working with a friend can be more fun!

There are several things you should do when you decide to work together.

First, listen to the other person's ideas.

Second, take turns talking and listening.

Third, share your tools, such as glue or paint, with everyone in the group.

Most importantly, be patient, kind, and **respectful** towards your teammates.

Working together is a great way to get the job done.

What Would You Do?

Find a partner (or two) and create your own book.

Pick one person to be the author. He or she will write the story.

Pick another person to be the illustrator. He or she will draw and color the pictures.

Work together to decide on a plot and characters.

Figure out how many pages you will need to tell your story.

Write and illustrate your story.

Staple the pages of your book together.

Don't forget to design the cover!

Picture Glossary

cooperate (koh-OP-uh-rate): To work with others on an activity.

goal (GOHL): A result someone wants and works for.

project (pra-JEKT): An activity that takes effort and planning.

respectful (ri-SPEKT-fuhl): To be polite and thoughtful to others.

talents (TAL-uhntss): Natural skills or abilities that you have.

teamwork (TEEM-wurk): The working together of a group of people.

Index

Websites

www.activities-for-kids.net/cooperation-activities-for-kids.html

freestoriesforkids.com/tales-for-kids/values-and-virtues/ stories-about-cooperation

www.goodcharacter.com/YCC/Cooperation.html

About the Author

Kyla Steinkraus lives in Tampa, Florida with her husband and two kids. She and her family practice working together when they cook dinner, put together a Lego set, or clean up the toy room.

Ask The Author!
www.rem4students.com